By Abraham Great

Copyright ©2013 Revised 2020

ISBN: 978-1-908040-26-8

Published in the UK by:

Golden Pen Publishing Ltd

All right reserved

Golden Pen (Publishing)

A Division of Golden Pen LTD

Milton Keynes,

United Kingdom

info@goldenpenpublishing.com

www.goldenpenpublishing.com

Cover design by Media Expression Intl (Check this )

Printed in the UK

# ABRAHAM GREAT

# 31 DECISIONS THAT MAKE A WOMAN OF VALUE

*Essential Values of a Great Woman*

# DEDICATION

I dedicate this book in memory of my late father Reverence Joshua Olukunle Akintayo who make a decision to fight for me to live to fulfil my own destiny.

The man who recognized that my name would be crucial to my destiny. Love you forever dad.

# INTRODUCTION

Despite the prevalence of patriarchal ideologies, women have proven time and again to the capable of offering value beyond the four walls of the kitchen and the bedroom. Our present world, as well as the ancient time have not failed to record exceptional feats achieved by the female folk in politics, business, science and even military.

This is because impact, value, talent, passion, determination and success are not gender specific words. However, none of these things work themselves out, they are all put to work by anyone who cares enough to show interest in them.

The difference between a mere woman and a woman of substance lies in the decisions they make (or refuse to make). Women who have proven to be valuable through the mark they have made in their world are those who have identified success factors and made a decision to engage them. They have risen above the waters of inherited gullibility and complacency in a world where the claim that it is a man's world continues to fly about.

The new millennium seemed to usher in the ripple effects of trailblazing feminine inspirations as more and more women continue to prove their mental emancipation to the world, yet there is still a long way to go as there countless women still yearn to know how to succeed at showing the world how much potentials lying beneath the alluring appeal of their delicate frame. The answer to their yearning is in knowing what to do regardless of their endeavours- that is-the decisions they must make.

This book is a compendium of thirty-one of such decisions. Some of these decisions appear simple and insignificant, but pregnant with so much effectiveness that once you begin to engage them one after the other, they will culminate in remarkable record of shift from being an ordinary woman to a shining example of excellence.

The possibility of living your best life and having all your dreams come true truly lies in the power of decisions. You do not express your choice just by mere words, but by your actions and attitudes. These are not automatic; they all begin with a decision. You are therefore implored to take seriously the content of this material and make it a point of obligation to follow through.

# ACKNOWLEDGMENT

My deepest appreciation goes to my wife! You have been a wonderful companion who have watch me make several decisions but follows with meekness. Your willingness to make a turn in the right direction with me every time we realized we might have made a wrong decision is commendable.

To my son, Abraham Darren Great, to you I owe the title of this book and the inspiration to write it. Thank you for the listening ears during those telephone conversations in the car, which eventually culminated into the idea behind this book. A leader you are, and that you will always be. To Dexter and Divine, thank you for being on your wisest behaviors each time daddy is busy teaching or writing. Finally, to Denzel who was not born was this book was first published, but whose positive energy helps me to get through making newness out of this second edition. You guys are Great.

This book would not have been available for print without the help of my Staff at Gr8terworks, HLBC and Golden Pen LTD – Thanks to all of your contributions. You guys are a great blessing and joy.

To an amazing Executive Manager at Golden Pen – Gabriel Olayemi, you work tirelessly on this manuscript to interpret my vision into concept, thank you for being a person and a man of value. Idris Babatunde – You have the great mind to capture words and interpret them appropriately, you too are a great asset, thank you for your work on this book.

To all HLBC members, I thank you for the privilege of serving as your leader, teaching these principles that work. Indeed, it is working. Finally,

# 31
# DECISION
# THAT MAKE
# A WOMAN OF
# VALUE

Life begins with decisions

Abraham Great

# CONTENT

# DECISION TO BE HAPPY

## 1. DECISION TO BE HAPPY

### "The prospect of the righteous is joy"
### Proverbs 10:28

W hat does happiness have to with decision? You may ask. Afterall, happiness is an emotion and decision is an act. A lot of people believe that happiness is inspirational; it comes and goes as it will.

Well, in reality, happiness- like other emotions- is well linked to decision. We may not realize it, but there are many times when we decide to be miserable. This means, we can also decide to be happy. It is all a matter of choice.

How can you decide to be happy? First is learning the truth about happiness. One of the greatest things you can learn in life is that happiness does not depend on outward circumstances. Happiness and its source lie within you, not outside of you. It comes from your heart. So the decision to be happy is tightly interlaced with the decision on what you let into your heart.

If you give the cares and fears of this world a place in your heart, you're blowing your chance at happiness. On the other hand, if you build up a foundation for your happiness by letting God into your heart, then you can be happy no matter what.

Why is happiness under your control? The reason is simple: it is not an event, but an attitude. You cannot possibly hope to control events, but you can always control your attitude towards them. One way to go about this is to resolve to be grateful in every situation. It's so much easier to be happy and content, when you are grateful even for the smallest of good things in your life. Be grateful for the woman God has made you become, for the home God has blessed you with, for the talent God has gifted you with to bless the world with.

If you stay grateful and positively tuned, you easily find pleasure and satisfaction even in the smallest things in life. Contentment is a great gift you can give yourself, whilst constant strife can exhaust you. It's hard to be happy, when you keep on thinking about what you do not have. If you're worried that you do not have a child yet, be grateful that you have a body and a womb ready for God's miracle at the set time. If you reason deeply, you'll realize sometimes that what you lack is much less in value than what you have. For example, instead of worrying that you don't have a car, why not be grateful for the legs? Cars come at a price, but your legs are priceless, irreplaceable. Therefore, make a decision to get focused on what you do have and give thanks for it.

The truth is that even God cannot make you happy. He can bless you, but the decision to be happy or not is yours. No matter how well you're blessed, if you're not content and grateful, you would still be unhappy. See, some people stay happy even while undergoing hard times in their lives, while others are unable to be happy no matter how much they have. It's all about choice

"Happiness is not something you postpone for the future; it is something you design for the present."

**Jim Rohn**

"God cannot give us a happiness and peace apart from Himself, because it is not there. There is no such thing."

**C. S. Lewis**

# DECISION TO LOVE

## 2. DECISION TO LOVE

**Let love and faithfulness never leave you; bind them around your neck, write them on the tablet of your heart. - Proverbs 3:3**

Love is the essence of life. These are not just fancy words. Love is something we all crave from our early childhood. Love is the only way life is possible. If you are a mother, you know how hard it can be to attend to a newborn baby. Still, love becomes the strongest motivation, a wind-like force that moves you to care and attend. Love is the only reason we survived being born as helpless babies totally dependent on others.

New mothers do not have to make a decision to love their babies. It comes naturally. Sadly, this does not play out when it comes to other people, especially those we are not familiar with, or are not so dear to us. This is not what we always get in life. This is why we have to make a decision to love other people. Granted, some people seem undeserving of it. Nevertheless, we have to make that decision because it is the right way to live.

Many of us are fortunate enough to be born in a loving family: Our parents shower us with love without reservations. But some people are not that lucky. They grew up in a hostile environment, one full of strife and resentment. But no matter what your background looks like, there is someone whose example you can follow - God. His love is perfect. What's more? He is love - the very source of love. If you let Him into your life with no reservations, He will teach you to follow after Him in loving others, including the seemingly unworthy ones.

Now, here is one important point: love is not a feeling. Yes, love is emotional, but it is not a feeling. Feelings come and go. They are ever changing like the sea. But love is an action, a resolve. And it is stable.

Also, love is unconditional. One of the greatest definitions of love is this: love covers many sins. It does not overlook sin. Love is not blind. But it does all it can to redeem or make up for those sins and forgive them. You see, God did not just shut His eyes to our sins; He paid for them. He cancelled covered them with His love.

If we have Him as our source, we can love others the same way. No one is perfect. That is another reason we need love. If we were perfect, we could live by justice alone. But we need love, we crave love and we die without love. And since we have received His love, we must share it too. Therefore, I urge you to love your neighbour, love your husband (or your husband to be), love your children and everyone around you.

The most amazing thing about love is that it multiplies and easily grows. You need only to start it. When you make a decision to love, you launch this love machine. No matter how much love you gives away, it gets refilled for you. It's one of the universal laws you can follow as a guide to life and living.

"Affection is responsible for nine-tenths of whatever solid and durable happiness there is in our lives."

**C. S. Lewis**


"I have found the paradox, that if you love until it hurts, there can be no more hurt, only more love."

**Mother Teresa**

# DECISION TO BE LOVABLE

## 3. DECISION TO BE LOVABLE

**"I love those who love me, and those who seek me find me." Proverbs 8:17**

As much as we all crave love, sometimes we make it hard for others to love us. Of course, true love is unconditional, it covers up our imperfections and rains us in spite of ourselves. Still, love is not a reason to pamper your sins or your unacceptable character traits. Let's take a look at some tips on how to be lovable without losing your true personality.

### POSITIVE ATTITUDE

One of the things you need to understand is that being lovable does not mean conforming to anybody's demands or standards. There are times when you need to stand your ground, even if it means you become hardly lovable to some people. Sometimes people view you as lovable if you always say "yes". But in certain circumsatnces, such an answer is impossible. Still, one of the things that make you lovable despite the circumstances is your attitude. It is not the "yes" or "no" you say that matters most times, it is how you say it. You do not say no in an unruly manner when you can do it politely. That is what makes the real difference. The good news is that attitude is something totally in your power. You may not have the power over circumstances, but you have the power over your attitude.

It's easy to love someone who preserves good attitude in their heart no matter what happens. It's much easier to love cheerful people, than to love the sullen ones. So, check out your attitudes and tune them up to become more loving.

## KINDNESS

If you make a decision to be lovable, you need to be kind to people.

There are many people in this world, who know how to judge others. Being kind singles you out from the crowd. It's the law of sowing and reaping. What you sow, that same thing you will reap. Be kind to others and they will be kind to you. Start from your family. I know you may love them already, but be more intentional about showing them kindness beyond what is already routine. Pay closer attention and be sensitive to their needs. In no time, you will notice them looking out for you even more than ever before. Extend this act to others too around you and you will reap the fruits.

## BEING AN ENCOURAGER

Be encouraging, if you make a decision to be lovable. You see, it's so easy for us to criticize. Encouraging and praising people can be harder. Again, it all comes down to your attitude. What do you see: the half empty glass or the half full glass? People love those who know how to see good things in them and encourage them. If your children are performing averagely or even poorly, support them in ways you can. I am not saying pamper them or pat them on the back. But doing and saying things to make them see that they can do better goes a long way in bringing out the best in them.

## LISTENING EARS

Learn listening to people. We all have something to say. Talking is much easier than listening. I mean active and attentive listening here. You do not just pretend to listen to people thinking over your own words or thoughts. You actively and sincerely listen to them and make efforts to stay interested in what they are saying. This is something that definitely makes you lovable.

"If you would be interesting, be interested, if you would be pleased, be pleasing, if you would be loved, be lovable, if you would be helped, be helpful."

**William Arthur Ward quotes**

"If you want to be loved, be lovable."

**Ovid**

# DECISION TO LET GO

## 4. DECISION TO LET GO

**"Let your eyes look straight ahead; fix your gaze directly before you." Proverbs 4:25**

People are able to live in society and understand each other, because we have so much in common. Even people from different countries or continents still share some common human traits. One of such traits is our inclination to acquire. We acquire various tangible assets, money, clothes, furniture, antiques, stamps, etc. But besides tangible assets all of us acquire such intangible assets as memories, offenses, fears or faith, sorrows or joys, bitterness or sweetness, etc.

Talking about making a decision to let go, we should consider going through all those intangible assets and letting go of some of them. Our mind has its attic, which sometimes gets stuffed with all sorts of things. Some of them are positive; being funny, pleasant, cute and innoxious; while others are negative; being offenses, resentments and other burdensome stuff that weigh us down.

The negative ones are things we have to let go as soon as we can. The sooner you get rid of your burdening baggage, the better your life becomes. How do you do it? Let us consider some tips.

### LOOK THROUGH YOUR TANGIBLE ASSETS

Sometimes it's hard for us to detect the things that weigh us down in our souls. It may be hard to spot the problem. One of the ways to start is to look through our tangible assets. The stuff at your home may well reflect your soul and mind condition. Have you cluttered your home with various things, making it hardly suitable for living? Start by decluttering your home. Believe it or not it will help you to move on to your mind and soul and declutter them too.

## MAKE A LIST

Writing things down is another great way to declutter your mind and soul. You may have some things in your mind's attic not suitable for sharing with other people. So, sit down and write them down on paper. This will help you to "unload" your brain and reduce the strain in it. Plus, by seeing them on paper, you may go through them and sort them out.

It will help you to set your priorities right and see where you need to make a decision to forgive or be forgiven. Therefore, take your time to clean your physical and emotional or mental attic and create more room for life and happiness inside of you.

"Some people believe holding on and hanging in there are signs of great strength. However, there are times when it takes much more strength to know when to let go and then do it."

**Ann Landers**


"Holding on is believing that there's only a past; letting go is knowing that there's a future."

**Daphne Rose Kingma**

# DECISION
# TO WAIT

## 5. DECISION TO WAIT

**"Do not say, 'I'll pay you back for this wrong!'**
**Wait for the LORD, and he will avenge you."**
**Proverbs 20:22**

There is no doubt that patience is one of the best virtues in life. At the same time, patience is one of the hardest virtues to acquire. Patience does not simply drop on your laps; you have to exercise it. A decision to be patient will save you from many troubles in life.

It's a common opinion that the youth lack in patience. We tend to make rash decisions when patience is not exercised. This accounts for why many of our regrettable mistakes were made while still young and agile. Patience is a part of wisdom. Once you learn to take a break and think things over, you make much wiser decisions.

Patience is a crucial quality for every woman. It allows you to build and preserve relationships. Mothers know how trying little children- as precious as they are- can get. But every coin has two sides and motherhood greatly helps to build up our patience. The decision to wait is a very conscious one- not subconscious. It never happens by chance. It is exercised by intention. It's a quality you have to decide to develop and cultivate into your personality.

To tell the truth, this can be tough, but the results are worth it. Just think about it: how many decisions have you made being impatient? How many of them have turned out all right? Not many, huh?

So, what are some of the practical tips on deciding and learning to wait? You may start with such easy things as controlling your physical manifestations of impatience. Controlling your emotions can be much harder. But if you learn to control your body first, you can make it easier First of all, start by controlling your breathing. When you get impatient, your breathing becomes fast and shallow. So, stop and start breathing deeply and slowly. Next, relax the muscles of your face. When you get impatient, your face muscles as well as that of the rest of your body get tense. Start by relaxing your facial muscles. If you can sit down or lay down try to relax your entire body, then do. This helps you to get your adrenaline under control and to calm down a bit.

Once you cease being agitated in your body, it becomes easier to manage your emotions and make a decision to wait.

"Life was always a matter of waiting for the right moment to act."

**Paulo Coelho**


"It is strange that the years teach us patience; that the shorter our time, the greater our capacity for waiting."

**Elizabeth Taylor**

# DECISION TO IMPROVE

## 6. DECISION ON TO IMPROVE

**How much better to get wisdom than gold, to get insight rather than silver! - Proverbs 16:16.**

Most women have some measure of discontentment about themselves. From physical features like looks, weight, hair; to character defects such as temper or other things pertaining to the our personalities. Now, discontent is a good thing if you know how to convert it into an improvement process. Otherwise, discontent may lead to low self-esteem and constant self-nagging.

So, how do you go about improving yourself? Take a look at some action points:

### START SMALL

The reason we fail to improve on ourselves sometimes is thinking too big. Thinking big is good. But when you plan a big self-improvement project, there are big chances you will fail it if not taken in bits. So, start small. Make a list of 3 small things you can improve on. For instance, you may want to get up 30 min earlier than you usually do. Or, you may want to spend fifteen minutes in prayer each morning. Perhaps you plan to work out fifteen minutes longer. Things are easier to put place when taken in bits. It makes your improvements more doable and more probable.

### DEVELOP SMALL AND USEFUL HABITS

Habits rule our lives. It's easy for us to do the things we get used to doing. We do not even take a second thought, when doing them. So, start by forming at least three small and useful habits. Make a habit to put things back to their places right away. Or, spent at least five minutes thinking something over before you make a decision.

## LOVE YOURSELF

You cannot hope to improve on anything , unless you learn to love yourself. Improvement is something you do with a thing or a person you care for. If you do not love yourself, you risk turning your improvement into a demolishing process. That's because you get harsh, beating up yourself. Unknowingly, you are setting out on a path of self condemnation and hopelessness.

## CHOOSE HAPPINESS

You know, happiness does not really depend on your circumstances. You can be happy, if you decide to be. Mother Teresa once said: "I asked God to give me happiness, but He said it's impossible. He can give you the blessing, but it's up to you to be happy or to be miserable." There is nothing you need to change in yourself to be happy today!

"Spend some time this weekend on home improvement; improve your attitude toward your family."

**Bo Bennett**

"Change is vital, improvement the logical form of change."

**James Cash Penney**

# DECISION TO EXERCISE

## 7. DECISION TO EXERCISE

**When you walk, your steps will not be hampered; when you run, you will not stumble - Proverbs 4:12**

It's unfortunate that our modern style of life is hypo dynamic in its essence. We do not move around enough to keep up the level of health and burn the consumed calories. That is why being overweight is one of the major banes of modern existence.

The decision to exercise can help you to prolong your life and make it more enjoyable. Yes, it's always hard to start exercising. Trainers have confirmed that the first two weeks of exercising can be the most trying period. But afterwards a habit gets formed. Your body gets into the habit of moving around much and getting a certain load of work. It gets over the pains in strained muscles. It is when you form this good habit that you start enjoying your workout.

You need a lot of motivation to cultivate the habit. So, one thing you can do is start working out in a group. This way you become not only motivated, but also accountable to other people. They encourage you to move on with your workouts. Plus, group workouts are fun and you get a chance to make new friends.

However, there are some healthy alternatives to exercising for those who hate to spend time in gyms doing nothing but sweating. For one you may start gardening. This is a pretty hard work, so you get plenty of working out there. The difference is that you do something useful instead of just sweating. You grow your veggies, save money for your family budget and get a new and useful hobby.

Or, you may get a new sporting hobby. You may enjoy horse riding, biking, hiking or some other activity, where you need to move a lot.

You can increase the body movement involved in your everyday life activities. For instance, you may walk up the stairs instead of taking an elevator. Or, you may park your car farther away from your work or shop and walk that distance. Or, just walk to any destination within the walking distance instead of driving there.

Staying active by working out allows you to stay healthy and good looking, too. If you decide to go with just basic exercising, do cardio workouts. They keep your heart healthy and increase blood and lymph circulation in your body. It also keeps your skin well-nourished and good looking.

"An early-morning walk is a blessing for the whole day."

**Henry David Thoreau**

"If we could give every individual the right amount of nourishment and exercise, not too little and not too much, we would have found the safest way to health."

**Hippocrates**

# DECISION TO TRUST

## 8. DECISION TO TRUST

**So that your trust may be in the LORD, I teach you today, even you. - Proverbs 22:19**

Trusting comes easy to us when we are young. Lots of people have open and willing hearts in their youth. However, with years trust comes harder for us, because we undergo plenty of painful experiences. A lot of disappointment from people we love, trust and look up to. Notwithstanding, we still need to trust if we must lead a blissful life.

One of the things you have to bear in mind is that no person is perfect. This means there always remains the risk that your trust can be betrayed. God is the one to be perfectly trusted, because He is perfect. He will never betray you or let you down.

Still, life becomes unbearable without trusting others. How can we build relationships with other people if we do not trust them? Let's learn some ways to restore trust, which is the essential ingredient of any healthy and purposeful relationship.

### TRUST IN THE PRESENT

Here is what I mean: Sometimes we fail to trust people we love because of the past offenses. Your man in the past may have betrayed your trust and so you have a hard time trusting in your current relationships. So, make sure your trust or hard feelings are relevant to the current situation. Trash the old baggages in the bin of the past. Do not allow them ruin your present.

## BE WISE TRUSTING

Making a decision to trust does not mean you become blind or gullibe. Of course, trust means you do not dig for bad things. Still, if you sense something sinister, then you have a timely alarm for you to be saved from the pain of false trust.

## TAKE A RISK

Remember, trust in people always involves a measure of risk. So, risk wisely. Again, do not equal risk of trust with blindness. Set boundaries, especially in new relationships. There is no total guarantee that you can't be hurt, but you would do well to give people the benefit of a doubt and let time reveal to you whether they merit it or not.

## BE TRUSTWORTHY

You cannot expect people to treasure your trust, if you break theirs. So, do your best to be a trustworthy person. Be willing to go an extra mile to avoid failing people's trust in you.

## GET RID OF PAIN

If someone has broken your trust, it may still hurt. So, you need to get healed in your heart to be able to restore your trust. Get proactive. Do not wait for time to heal the wounds. Look for solutions and ways to get rid of the pain for the sake of your sanity.

As you may see, all these things may help you to make a decision to trust and build up great and loving relationships in your life.

"The best way to find out if you can trust some-body is to trust them." **Ernest Hemingway**

"The best proof of love is trust." **Joyce Brothers**

DECISION 9

# DECISION
# TO FORGIVE

## 9. DECISION TO FORGIVE

**"But with you there is forgiveness, so that we can, with reverence, serve you." - Psalms 130:4**

Forgiveness does not always come natural, but it is a process made possible with a decision. Forgiveness is a process. Only a few people find forgiveness easy; it's a hard thing for most of us. However it comes for us, it certainly holds a great deal of benefits for you and the ones you forgive. Let's take a look at some of them.

### FORGIVENESS OPENS UP A WAY

Often times, resentment and offenses creates obstacles in your life. This wall is invisible, but very real. It blocks relationships, opportunities, success and even health. Living with resentment in your heart makes you blind to new opportunities and people. It does not only block the relationships with the people you do not forgive, but it also blocks new relationships from developing. You become afraid to start new relationships or you simply do not have enough room in your heart to accommodate more people.

### FORGIVENESS BRINGS FREEDOM

Do you know who suffers the most from being unforgiving? The one who fails to forgive! If you hold the bitterness and resentment in your heart, these feelings torture you. These are strong feelings capable of not only destabilizing you emotionally, but also ruining your physical health. They gnaw at you and make your life unbearable.

So, forgiveness is the way to freedom. You free your heart from negative feelings and make room in it for positive ones. You also free the other person from the bondage created by your resentment towards them. Most of the times neither of you need that bondage in life.

## FORGIVENESS BRINGS HEALING

It heals you from inside out. It heals your heart and eventually it relieves the strain and stress from your body. Most of the times you cannot forgive just by making a will or mind decision, but you have to forgive anyway, for your heart to heal. In most cases, bitter feelings abide and deep down in your heart, forgiveness is a process you need to go through to set yourself free and be healed from them. However, it starts with your decision to forgive.

## *FORGIVENESS SAVES YOU TIME

If you could count all the time you have spent going through all those heavy feelings and thoughts refusing to forgive, you would be amazed. These negative inner conversations and hard feelings can consume hours, days or even years of your life. So, forgiveness saves you time and provides you with a chance to live a happier life. It's a good thing to examine your heart right now and start the forgiveness process by making the decision to forgive and let go of past offenses.

"It takes a strong person to say sorry, and an ever stronger person to forgive."

**Unknown**


"People are often unreasonable and self-centered. Forgive them anyway."

**Mother Teresa**

# DECISION NOT TO BE BITTER

## 10. DECISION NOT TO BE BITTER

**Above all else, guard your hear t , for everything you do flows from it. - Proverbs 4:23**

Bitterness is dangerous! It seems to be an insignificant feeling, but it has the potential of ruining your entire life. One of the reasons bitterness is dangerous is that it strikes your heart. It starts like a small thing. At first it may even sort of spice up your life, as bitter herbs do with the food.

However, bitterness has one dangerous property: it can grow. It grows slowly like cancer. If you do not guard your heart against bitterness or let it stay there undetected, you let it grow there. Growing up it eats up your heart. For a while, like tumor, bitterness may not cause any trouble. But once it crosses the limit, it turns your life into hell.

It starts to rule all your emotions and thoughts; consequently, it takes over your actions and your entire life. The larger the bitterness grows, the harder it is to get rid of it. So, the best decision you can make is to search your heart now for any bitterness and get rid of it when it is still small.

There are many cases in life, when people let their bitterness grow for years. It breaks down their relationships with other people. It leads them to court after causing them to commit serious crimes like murder. So, bitterness is no joke. When finally people get help, forgive and get rid of their bitterness, they usually do not even remember how it all started.

Furthermore, bitterness is contagious. It is transferrable from one person to another. A bitter person can share negative opinions with others about something or someone. When accepted, it spreads. Hence, while making the decision not to be bitter, you should also guard yourself and make a decision to stay away from bitter people. They are contagious.

On the other hand, bitterness can be conquered by love. This is the strongest antidote to bitterness and love is also contagious. Make a decision to love in your heart, in your words and in your actions, and you can stay protected from bitterness.

"Bitterness imprisons life; love releases it."

**Harry Emerson Fosdick**

"Never succumb to the temptation of bitterness".

**Martin Luther King, Jr.**

# DECISION TO BE INDEPENDENT

## 11. DECISION TO BE INDEPENDENT

### "My salvation and my honor depend on God" - Psalm 62:7

Independence is a tricky concept. Making a decision to be independent can benefit you hugely, but it can also ruin your life. It all depends on how you go about this decision and what you understand by independence.

You may hear people talk about being self-sufficient and independent. It's a new trend in popular culture. You need to be "self-sufficient" and proudly independent to fit in. However, no one can be truly selfsufficient and independent just because it's not the way we were created. Independence is a very relative concept. We were created to be dependent on God. There is a strong inner craving in each and every one of us. We crave to be loved, accepted, supported. If we were meant to be independent, why were we not left alone after being born? Why would we get born into a family?

You know, family is all about mutual dependence and help, isn't it? Independence is a good thing within reasonable boundaries. The problem is that many people try to cross those boundaries. And since they cannot reach for that total independence they aim for, it creates emptiness. This is where addiction may set in- a substitute to fill up the void created by desperation to be independent. All addictions rule human lives. They occupy the empty place in the hearts of people and this emptiness can be filled in only by one Presence- the presence of God. That is the only true and positive addiction we can live with and a positive dependence we should aim for. So, when making a decision to be independent, you should remember that no man is an island. Living in a family, in a church or in other social environments is an evidence of the need for mutual dependence. Husbands depend on their wives, so do wives depend on their husbands. This does not rule out personal independence. Independence is needed in areas such as your thinking. You should not allow others' thought sway you out of sound reasoning. It's good to be independent, when it is about taking care of your own basic needs.

It's great to be independent, when you need to make the right decision and go against the flow to stand for the truth. It's awesome to be independent, when you carry a load of responsibility for other people, for your family, etc. But the roots of such independence and ability to hold on to what you believe to be the truth lie deep in your dependence upon God. When you get addicted to Him, no outward addiction can get hold of you. You become truly independent and sufficient.

"If money is your hope for independence you will never have it. The only real security that a man will have in this world is a reserve of knowledge, experience, and ability."

**Henry Ford**

"Independence? That's middle class blasphemy. We are all dependent on one another, every soul of us on earth."

**George Bernard Shaw**

# DECISION TO INVEST

## 12. DECISION TO INVEST

**"One person gives freely, yet gains even more; another withholds unduly, but comes to poverty." - Proverbs 11:24**

Sometimes, when we hear the word "investment", we think of money only. However, making a decision to invest is not limited by financial issues. The word 'investment' is tightly bound with the word "growth". Do you have the areas of your life, where you need growth? Then think of investing into them.

You see, this is one of the laws of our life: when you invest, growth takes palce. The more you invest into something, the more it grows. Sometimes we become focused on saving, instead of investing. Saving is a good thing, but it does not make anything grow. When you try to save money, you just accumulate them bit by bit, but you do not make them grow into a fortune. Saving is good, but investment is better.

One of the best areas to invest in is YOU. You are worth an investment. You may not have any investors presently in your life. But you can always become your biggest investor. See, investment takes faith, because for every investment, returns are expected. Hence, making a decision to invest in yourself starts by keeping up your faith in you. You are worth your investment. Start by investing your time. Some people invest their time in others, in their lives and their projects, but they grudge the time for themselves.

If you want to make your life grow, you need to invest time in your health, your education, knowledge, self development, your career, your family, etc. You cannot expect your life to grow by some miracle, if you do not invest in it.

Gandhi once said that we should learn and gain new knowledge as if we are meant to live forever. It's a good rule to go by. Sometimes, we limit our investment into learning just because we think we'd never have use for that knowledge. If that is the case with you, take time and invest it into paradigm shift. Develop a new approach to life and it will pay back with rich dividends of success and growth.

Also, make a decision to take time and invest in other people, too. It does not mean you have to invest money. You may invest your time, your love, your support and your faith in them. Such investments bring high Returns On Investment in time of need.

"An investment in knowledge pays the best interest."

**Benjamin Franklin**

"Always invest for the long term."

**Warren Buffett**

# DECISION 13

# DECISION TO BE CLEAN

## 13. DECISION TO CLEAN

**Who can say, "I have kept my heart pure; I am clean and without sin?" - Proverbs 20:9**

K eeping your body clean, tidy and well-tended is a good idea. Physical cleanliness is not an issue for most people today. Maintaining your physical cleanliness requires efforts, but keeping yourself clean inside can be a more challenging task.

Have you ever seen a nice, clean, good smelling person? You like their looks, they seem to be such nice, and gorgeously dressed until... they open up their mouth and speak. You hear them speak and you sense that inner filth coming out of them like a stench. There are so many things that can contaminate us inwardly, and none of them can be covered up in physical cleanliness.

So, making a decision to keep your heart clean is one of the key decisions in life. This decision determines the course of your life and the end of your life. It is a choice between curse and blessing. How do you keep yourself clean from the inside? You need to clean up your soul time after time and avoid letting filth accumulate there.

And, of course, you need to make right the choices on what you let come inside of you. Your eyes and your ears are the gateway to your soul. Watch what you hear and see; open your eyes and tune your ears. Be careful as to who you listen to and what opinions you allow to nest in your mind and heart. Such things as movies, TV, books, newspapers, the Internet, are all sources of nutrient or filth for your soul. You need to be able to monitor what things you let in your soul. Do not watch programmes or read literatures telling women that submission to their husband is absurd. Those are not scriptural. You also need to monitor what you let out of yourself. The things you let out are evidences of what you have let in. Your words are the mirrors of your heart. If the words are filthy, then the heart is filthy, too.

The only way to clean the words is by cleaning the heart first. The ultimate cleaning can be done only by the Most High. But you owe the duty to make daily decisions on staying clean inside and guarding the gateway of your soul.

"I will not let anyone walk through my mind with their dirty feet."

**Mahatma Gandhi**

"Take care of your body. It's the only place you have to live."

**Jim Rohn**

# DECISION TO CREATE ORDER

## 14. DECISION TO CREATE ORDER

**"Put your outdoor work in order and get your fields ready; after that, build your house." - Proverbs 24:27**

O rder is something most of us struggle with. You may have a perfect house, clean and well organized, this is just one of the many things in your life in which order is of the essence. In fact, there is not aspect of life where order can be done away with - work, leisure, daily routine, thoughts, speech and every other thing you can think of. Order is simply the way you arrange things in relation to each other to prevent chaos or confusion.

### START SMALL

You have already read about this advice in earlier chapters. Well do not be bored of it because its effectiveness cannot be overemphasized. It works a great deal. Let's say you have a messy house and you make a decision to put it to order. The task can be overwhelming. Most likely you'd get depressed thinking of all the mess you have to clean. You get frustrated and end up losing any desire to get to work.

So, what do you do? Start small. Get an alarm clock and set it for fifteen minutes. Then pick one small area of your house and clean hard for the set time. You know, you can make yourself do almost anything for fifteen minutes. When the alarm sounds, take a break and start the whole process over again. Make it a new habit.

### PRIORITIZE

Sometimes we get confused about our tasks. We do not know where to start from. And there are so many people or trends in the world, which tell us what things should go first.

They may not be right. Who can know your life priorities better then you? So, free your head and heart from all the you-must-do things and from the opinions of other people. Now you are ready to put together a list of your own priorities. If you have a number of things you wish to achieve in the next five years, order them in a list of preferences. Let's say you want to further your education, advance your career, by a home and start having children, you start with what is most urgent, and able to give you the leverage to obtain and sustain the next.

You can start with your education, knowing it will propel you to a status that qualifies for a better job or a promotion. You can then proceed to start paying for a house after some time, just to make sure that the expanded financial responsibility that comes with raising children does not tell on your home acquisition. You may not necessarily follow this order. As stated before, you are in the best position to determine your priorities. Just do what would work best for you by putting your endeavours in order.

## STOP THE RUSH

We all get rush hours in our lives. For some people, mornings are the busiest time of their day. It's very hard to create order, when you are in a hurry. So, do some planning and try to slow down your rush hour a bit. Make a list of all the things you can do ahead of time and do them. This would help you to avoid hurry and havoc in the peak time.

## DECLUTTER

Often times it is hard to for us to decide and create order just because we have so much clutter in our lives. It can be a physical clutter in your house, or it can be some emotional or mental clutter. Start decluttering your life. Throw away or give away all the things you do not need at your home. Deal with such emotions as offense, bitterness, unforgiveness. This is the emotional trash you have no use for in your life. Having done that, you can now begin to order the good thoughts worth focusing on.

"Good order is the foundation of all great things."

**Edmund Burke**


"Order marches with weighty and measured strides. Disorder is always in a hurry."

**Napoleon Bonaparte**

# DECISION TO TRY

## 15. DECISION TO TRY

**The lot is cast into the lap, but its every decision is from the LORD. - Proverbs 16:33**

Some of us may feel that the life has fallen into a well-trodden path and it becomes monotonous. We get bored and strive for change. But what keeps up back? Why is making a change or trying something new so hard? Let's try to understand what holds us back and how we can make and keep the decision to try.

### FEAR

Fear is one of the things that hold us back from trying new things. Scientists have discovered that people dread the unknown. Yes, we may fear the things that surely do not turn out well, but we dread the unknown outcomes. We may fear less what we foreknow, but really dread unknown outcomes. And it is mostly subconscious.

We simply do not realize it with our conscious minds. We just feel the discomfort or experience lack of motivation to do new things. Bringing that fear out and comprehending it may be the first step to make in overcoming it. Confronting your fear of the unknown is the first decision to make, when you wish to try something new.

### HABIT

This is another vicious hindrance against trying new things. We all develop habits in life. Once we develop them, we tend to carry on for long. So, a good way to go about teaching yourself to try new things is to develop a habit. Some of us are complacent; we are quick to put off something new. It is not a good habit. And the best way to stop a bad habit is to replace it with a good one. Cultivate the habit trying things now. Get yourself in a habit of preferring new things to the well tried ones. It starts with small things, such as picking new dishes at a restaurant; watching new movies or reading new books, etc.

Once you train yourself and develop a habit of trying new things, it becomes really easy and comfortable. Do not be afraid of mistakes. They may be awkward at first, but they help learn to do things better. When we try something new, we always have that question coming up in our minds: what if I won't like it? What if I fail? So what? But I urge you to try first and see the outcome and not just jump to discouraging conclusions. Your life does not have to consist of successes or right choices only. You need to let yourself make mistakes, learn and even enjoy them!

"Defeat is not the worst of failures. Not to have tried is the true failure."

**George E. Woodberry**

"Only those who dare to fail greatly can ever achieve greatly."

**Robert F. Kennedy**

# DECISION
# TO GIVE

## 16. DECISION TO GIVE

**One person gives freely, yet gains even more; another withholds unduly, but comes to poverty. - Proverbs 11:24**

Giving and receiving are the two natural processes of life. However, there are cases in our lives when giving becomes hard. There are times when giving does not feel like the reasonable thing to do. Nevertheless, giving is a habit we must cultivate. It has to be a lifestyle. On this note, let us address some factors that make giving difficult so we know how to cross them out.

### FEAR

One of the reasons people find it hard to give is fear. Fear can paralyze you from inside out. You plan to give, but then fear seizes your heart and your emotions. You become afraid that if you give, you will lack. Fear is not the best advisor in life. If you have made a decision to give, you need to confront your fear. Look it in the eye so to say. Sometimes you may just have to give in spite of your fear. It might be the only way to overcome it. You get positive experience giving and the fear goes away.

### LACK OF TRUST

This is another reason people are reluctant to give. You may feel the call of God to give, but if you do not trust God completely, you have a hard time giving. You become afraid that He will not take care of you. You hold back on loving your husband the way you ought to, because you are afraid it will not be reciprocated. Why not trust on God to take charge of his heart? If you wish to become a giver, you need to learn to trust in God.

## STINGINESS

This is one seriously disadvantageous character defect. Most of us do not like to admit we have it. How can you watch your fellow human being suffer for things you can afford to give and not feel guilty about it? It is not that you do not have, you just lack the compassion and willingness. There is no way to cure stinginess other than putting yourself in people's shoes help them as much as you can afford to. Still, a decision to give is the only cure for it.

Now, giving is not only about money. You can give your time, your efforts, your 'ears' to listen someone who needs it. You can make a long list of things you may give. You may have a gift of giving wise counsel. But how can you know if you cant give listening ears to a fellow woman who is facing challenges in her family and career? Love is the best guide for giving. If you love people, it becomes easy for you to see, where their needs are and how you can meet them. You may feel that you have needs too, but giving sacrificially is even more worthy. Jesus would not have been sacrificed for our sins if God had not so loved the world.

Generosity is another attribute of giving. God is generous. He always gives us more than enough. We should follow in His footprints. You see, the secret of giving is that you free the room in your life for receiving. This is how you avoid stagnation in life. If you feel life your life has become some-what stale, make a decision to give.

"Let us not be satisfied with just giving money. Money is not enough, money can be got, but they need your hearts to love them. So, spread your love everywhere you go."

**Mother Teresa**

"I have found that among its other benefits, giving liberates the soul of the giver."

**Maya Angelou**

# DECISION TO RECEIVE

## 17. DECISION TO RECEIVE

### ...and receive favor from the LORD - Proverbs 8:35

Some people believe that giving is more spiritual and moral than receiving. But that is not true. What can you give, if you do not receive first? When we are born, we receive for many years and later start giving back. There is nothing shameful in receiving.

It's also a common belief that only strong people give and weak people receive. Receiving is not a weakness. It's a necessity. You do not say that people who eat or drink are weak. We have to eat, drink, sleep or breathe. All these things are necessities.

The key in making a decision to receive is to maintain a balance between giving and receiving. Many women tend to give. They give their love, care and hard work to their families. They build a career by giving their best at work. You deserve to receive care too, after so much of you that you have given. Today's culture puts a high strain on women, a demand to be strong. Since many view receiving as weakness, women become loath.

It's great when you can receive from others who see your need and give help willingly. But there are cases when you have to ask for help. One of the ways to make a decision to receive is to get rid of false beliefs. "Ask and you will be given", said Jesus. There are times when we have to ask for things to receive them.

Prayer is one of the great ways to get refilled and to receive a favour from the Lord. But remember asking requires humility, but not humiliation. Yes, you do have to humble yourself to ask and to receive. But the Lord never humiliates you by wanting you to ask from Him.

The same is true about asking and receiving from people. There is a huge difference between humility and humiliation. You have to understand it to receive and be thankful.

We all need help from time to time. There are no perfect people on Earth. So, be willing to humble yourself and receive help, when you need it. You need help with loads of house chores, ask. You are a bit short on cash to buy gas to fuel you car, ask. Having been good enough to give so much, do not hesitate to receive help with open arms because this is how you also get refilled to give again.

> "Asking is the beginning of receiving. Make sure you don't go to the ocean with a teaspoon. At least take a bucket so the kids won't laugh at you."

**Jim Rohn**


> "Women tend to have recognition and peer group support - recognition from friends and family that this has to be a big issue in their lives. They're more comfortable expressing the need for support and receiving it."

**James Levine**

# DECISION TO LIVE A BALANCED LIFE

## 18. DECISION TO LIVE A BALANCED LIFE

**"The Lord detests dishonest scales, but accurate weights find favour with him" -
Proverbs 11:1**

Making a decision to live a balanced life does not mean you have to dedicate equal amounts of time or efforts to all aspects of your life. This can really be an uphill task. A balanced life means giving an adequate amount of time, money or efforts to different things in your life. Again this decision is tightly bound by the decision to priorities your life.

Again, the fast pace of life makes balancing very challenging. Some people feel as if they have turned into some kind of circus acrobats, who spin the plates on sticks holding them in their hand, on one foot and even on the nose. Have you seen those? It seems like you do maintain balance, but how long can you last?

Living a well-balanced life gives you time and opportunity to rest, to restore your strength and enjoy your life. A well-balanced life is a stress free life. We all experience a lot of stress, but there comes a line, which should not be crossed. If you cross that line, you become overstrained and misbalanced.

Again, you need to set up your priorities right to attain a balanced life. Top priorities demand more of your time and attention. You need to learn to turn off the sound of those urgent (but not important) and loud things to reduce your level of stress.

And the way to live a balanced life? Plan in advance. Things tend to get crowded at a certain point of your life. Most of us experience rapid stress in the morning. There are so many things you need to attend to. It seems impossible to fit them all in one short morning and start the day in a good mood. Making a decision to balance your life you can do something about such rush hours of your life.

For instance, you're getting the children ready for school, and at the same time, getting adequately prepared for the pitch scheduled for early morning. To maintain your balance, you may do some things in the evening- like all the kitchen chores that usually get done in the morning to make your morning hours are less stressful. Plan other activities that follow that same evening ahead of the next day. Write down the things that need to be done tomorrow. This way you free up your mind from staying focused on these upcoming events or problems and you allow yourself to rest better during the night. This is how you practically balance up your life and free up your rush hours a bit.

The key to living balanced life is adequate planning. This you must decide in order to live your best life.

"The major work of the world is not done by geniuses. It is done by ordinary people, with balance in their lives, who have learned to work in an extraordinary manner."

**Gordon B. Hinckley**

"Happiness is not a matter of intensity but of balance, order, rhythm and harmony."

**Thomas Merton**

DECISION 19

# DECISION TO HOPE

## 19. DECISION TO HOPE

**There is surely a future hope for you, and your hope will not be cut off. - Proverbs 23:18**

Hope is a tricky word to write about. Hope has become the theme for many poets and writers; it has been romanticized, somewhat. Still, hope remains a very practical thing. It's like a rope we hang on to in tough times in life. The analogy is seems alluded to in the Bible verse "hope will not be cut off."

The rope in itself is neither good nor bad. Just like rope, it is a question of what it is tied to. If you hang over a deep gap, you would surely prefer to have that rope tied up to something strong and able to hold you. This is important to understand, when we talk about making a decision to hope. A vain hope will not help you in making it through life.

Therefore, very importantly, your hope must be tied to the truth. If you tie your hopes to a wrong thing, they would fail you. You see, it's a good decision to view your hope as an investment. Most of us are pretty careful, taking a lot into consideration when it comes to investing our money. But few of us are that careful when it comes to investing our hopes, whereas investment of hope is crucial one in your life. Most of us resort to hope, when we go through tough times. Hope stimulates us to move on and many of us would have been completely lost or quit if not for our hopes. But when you are already hanging over a gap for too long, it may eventually get too late to try and tie your rope onto something solid.

You need to make a decision find the truth of God's word to tie your rope to, while the going is good; so that if it ever gets tough, it won't fail you. View your hope as your investment and find right foundations for it. Investing your hope in the Most High is the best decision you can make.

"Hope is the thing with feathers
That perches in the soul
And sings the tune without the words
And never stops at all."

**Emily Dickinson**

"Only in the darkness can you see the stars."

**Martin Luther King Jr.**

# DECISION TO LOVE YOURSELF

## 20. DECISION TO LOVE YOURSELF

**"Let love and faithfulness never leave you; bind them around your neck, write them on the tablet of your heart." - Proverbs 3:3**

Loving yourself is not selfish. Jesus Christ said: love others as you love yourself. It basically means you cannot love others more than you love yourself. It means there is the place of loving yourself. In fact, that saying indicates that you love yourself first, then out of the abundance of self-love, you extend to your neighbour. It is not even possible to love your neighbour right, if you do not love yourself enough. You cannot treat them better than you treat yourself. So, if you have certain relationship problems, it probably stems from not loving yourself enough.

Now, let's talk of what self-love is. It's not what they advertise on TV. There are thousands of ads trying to convince you that you are worth something. They motivate you to go ahead and spend money on something. They patronize you, so you can patronize them. But that is not love. Spending more than you can afford on highly prized accessories and adornment in the bid to look your best does not mean you love yourself. Any kind of love includes discipline. If you love yourself, you discipline yourself with regard to money, food, exercise, etc.

You need to love yourself enough to be able to say no to your desires and cravings. Overspending, overeating and other superfluities have nothing to do with true self-love. So now you know, discipline is one of the ingredients of self-love.

Also, you must care and plan. Many women out there totally exhaust themselves. They work, work and work. They have the day job, they have the house to manage, they have their husband and their kids to attend to. After all this comes themselves as put list themselves last. And it may never get to them because all others listed are hardly fully satisfied. But do not try to be a perfectionist. Do not best, but do not try to perfectly satisfy others' concerns at your expense. In the process of doing this, many women have become a shadow of themselves; some have fallen; some have even given up the ghost. If you love yourself, you need to maintain a proper balance between serving others and serving yourself. You need to plan your rest time. You need to attend to your diet and sleep. Self-care is one of the essential elements of self-love.

It's okay to have some time just for yourself. You may spend some time at leisure, doing nothing or doing something you really enjoy, even if it has no practical value for other people. This is how you get refreshed. If you do not spend time resting or enjoying life, you turn into a 'nagzila', nagging your family all the time, discontent and unhappy. The saying is very true: if mom is not happy, the whole family is not happy.

Finally, spend time in prayer and in the Word of God. There is nothing as refreshing as this. You need to renew your emotions and your spiritual strength, as you do your body. So, set aside a sacred time just for you and God. This is the most important relationship in your life, therefore maintain it.

"You have to be able to love yourself because that's when things fall into place."

**Vanessa Hudgens**

"If you don't love yourself, you can't love anybody else. And I think as women we really forget that."

**Jennifer Lopez**

# DECISION
# TO DECLUTTER

## 21. DECISION TO DECLUTTER

**"If you find honey, eat just enough - too much of it, and you will vomit." - Proverbs 25:16**

Too much of anything is not good. Clutter has more to it then you think. It eats up your life. Just think of it for a moment: what is it you lack the most in your life? For many women out there, it is free time. They get too busy with other things. There is no time to rest, to play, to read, to be happy. Now, why should you declutter?

Well, clutters eat up your time. Clutters come in different forms. You may have too many things in your home, or you may have outdated emotions, unhealthy relationships, thoughts or convictions. All these things clutter people's lives and eat up their time. Remember the time you developed bitter feelings for someone? Just recall how much time you spent thinking or feeling them over and over again. Can you account for those times with gains to show?

Now that you know how wasteful clutters are, how do you start decluttering? Start with physical things. It's always easier. You know, our physical and spiritual lives are tied together. If you declutter your home, you open up the way to declutter your soul, too. Make decluttering a habit. Make a decision to declutter daily for a set duration. Just run through your house and pick ten things you do not need. Then make a decision to give them away or to throw them away.

Detect your 'hot clutter spots'. We all have them. You may notice a particular corner of your home, where the clutter seems to settle down. Or, you may see a small table cluttered with old newspapers, magazines or books. Or, you may stuff your clothes on a particular chair or sofa in your home. Go through your house and detect all such clutter zones. Make a list of them and start decluttering from these hot spots.

Declutter them first and then keep a sharp eye on them. Whenever you see stuff getting piled up on those hot spots, clean it right then and there. If you are not the only one who uses those clutter zones, talk about them to your family. You may even get radical and remove the table, chair or sofa for a while. This would surely send a strong message to your family.

Then move on to your thoughts and emotions. Find the hot clutter spots there and do away with them. It may be anger and unforgiveness for example- you discover people get you angry easily and hold so many people in your heart in resentment. Declutter. Free up emotional space for love and tolerance to flood in.

"Have nothing in your houses that you do not know to be useful, or believe to be beautiful."

**William Morris' Golden Rule:**


the More You Have...: "The more you have, the more you are occupied. The less you have, the more free you are."

**Mother Teresa**

# DECISION TO BE A FRIEND

## 22. DECISION TO BE A FRIEND

### "A friend loves at all times" - Proverbs 17:17

A decision to have friends is a good one, but a decision to be a friend is even better. It's not always in your power to decide and have good friends, but it is always in your power to decide to be a good friend. Even when there are no people around you and you feel lonely, there is an opportunity for friendship. You can always decide to be a friend of God. It is the most fulfilling friendship you can have in your life.

Now, there is a big difference between the two above mentioned decisions. We all want to have something, including having friends. It's so nice to have good friends, but how about deciding to BE a friend? When you have friends, you receive, but when you become a friend, you give. That's the major difference. Lots of people out there are prepared to receive, but few are ready to give.

You know, having friends is not a responsibility, but a benefit. But being a friend is a responsibility you take upon yourself. It's easy to be a friend of a happy person. But things change. All people have good times and bad times in their life. The true friends are those, who stick with you during the bad times. So, if you make a decision to be a friend, you have to be prepared to help people. You need to stick with them through the bad times and help them sustain the good ones.

You also have to be prepared to love them at all times. We all have shortcomings. So, if you make a decision to be a friend, you need to cover up the shortcomings of that person with your love. Plus, being a friend means you have to develop trust. Trusting people is risky. None of us can guarantee others' total loyalty. We all break trust time to time. So, if you make a decision to be a friend, you need to be ready to trust, while you also become trustworthy.

By making a decision to be a friend, you also make a decision to invest your time into friendship. You have to spend time with that person and share your companionship. This rush world and fast tempo of living makes it challenging. Still, it's a commitment you make and it is your responsibility to keep it.

Having shared with you so many things you need to do to become a friend, I believe you now realize that friendship has rich rewards to offer and it is well worth the investment.

"A friend is one who knows you and loves you just the same."

**Elbert Hubbard**

"A true friend never gets in your way unless you happen to be going down."

**Arnold H. Glasow**

# DECISION TO BE THANKFUL

## 23. DECISION TO BE THANKFUL

### "Sacrifice thank offerings to God, fulfill your vows to the Most High." - Psalm 50:14

There is a parable of two angels sent by God on collection missions. One was sent to collect petitions and the other one to collect thanks. The first one came back with a full basket of petitions and the other one came with just two thanks in the basket. This shows that the world is full of needy people. But thankful folks are few. One great thing about being thankful is that it prevents you from becoming bitter. Gratitude is an attitude. Unlike circumstances, attitudes are completely in your power. You can always manage them and change them.

Whereas circumstances do not have to dictate attitude, attitude changes circumstances. Sometimes we do tend to get grouchy and discontent. This leads to constant blaming and nagging of the people around us. Such negative attitudes may lead to some negative and greatly undesirable consequences. The home is where most people express discontent. People feel free to express ourselves at home and bitterness is one of the feelings we lash out there. Many women accuse their husbands of not giving them enough support; the children suffer criticism for not being perfect. Some ladies blame their parents for how they have not turned out to be the best they hoped to be in life. They do not know that every situation in the present is a step that potentially leads to something better. It is time for you to decide to be appreciate of your folks' efforts and God's blessings.

It's true that you may be in difficult circumstances and especially in your family. Believe me, there are no perfect husbands in the world. There is no perfect child. The same way there are no perfect wives. But gratitude can work miracles. It's not a good idea to nag or try to change your husband. The better idea is to make a decision to be thankful. When you become grateful for the things in your life, bitterness goes away and gets replaced with happiness and peace.

Another great thing about being thankful is that it shifts your perspective. It changes the way you see things. Many a time, that is all you really need. When you change the way you view things, you cease feeling the need to change them. Many things become acceptable or at least tolerable to you, when you stay thankful. To carry out the decision to become thankful, start by putting together a thank list. Write down at least 10 things you are grateful for. These can be such key things as your health, or little things as every meal you have.

Make gratitude your habit. Get in the habit of thanking God and people. Most of us pray for needs, because things hurt us or because we have urgent situations on hand. But once things get fixed up and pain or discomfort go away, we simply forget to say thank you. So, make a decision to become a profoundly thankful and content person.

"As we express our gratitude, we must never forget that the highest appreciation is not to utter words, but to live by them."

**John F. Kennedy**

"Gratitude is the fairest blossom which springs from the soul."

**Henry Ward Beecher**

# DECISION TO DRESS WELL

## 24. DECISION TO DRESS WELL

### "She is clothed with strength and dignity; she can laugh at the days to come." - Proverbs 31:25

See, the old saying goes: they meet you by your clothes, but they treat you by your mind. This means that our appearance does make a difference. You can never hope to make the first impression twice. And that first impression is mainly made by your looks.

Of course, the Bible does tell us that the key value of any person lies inside, not the outside. Appearance and beauty can be a false criteria to judge by. Still, if you wish to make an impression on other people, you need to pay attention to your appearance. Now, the Bible verse at the top of this chapter states: She is clothed with strength and dignity. It does not talk exactly about fashion or clothes, but it gives the idea of the style of the "perfect and godly woman". If it all you are that good inside, you should outwardly express it by the way you appear.

So, how should you pick your clothes? Should you make a decision to dress well? You certainly should. Because your style in clothes is one of the things that express your inner being.

See, dressing up has its place in life. We live in a consumer culture. We constantly are urged to consume more and more, with products and clothes probably top of the list. It's not the best idea to be guided by the brands in your style of dressing. This style is yours and it has to express well your inner self and not someone's ideas on what is fashionable and what is not. What is important is that you through your dressing exude dignity, beauty, modesty.

Therefore, keep yourself neat and fittingly dressed. Style includes such concept as appropriateness. It's not enough to look good in your clothes. If you make a decision to dress well, you need to dress fit for the occasion. You may put on something alluring, when you are with your husband, but a skimpy dress is not the best attire for church, school meeting or shopping.

The ability to bind together your inner content and your outer style and make it matching for the occasion is the best of what you do in deciding to dress well and look presentable.

"Clothes make the man. Naked people have little or no influence on society."

**Mark Twain**

"Beauty is ten, nine of which is dressing."

**Proverbs**

# DECISION TO SPEAK RIGHT THINGS

## 25. DECISION TO SPEAK RIGHT THINGS

**"You have been trapped by what you said, ensnared by the words of your mouth." - Proverbs 6:2**

Today, many people, women inclusive, have lost the faith in the power of word- if they ever had the faith at all. They do not think that what they say is really a big deal. They say good things or bad things, and then say it's joke, not believing that these words have consequences in their lives or the lives of those around them.

Our modern culture has devaluated these powers. The saying goes: believe none of the words you hear and only half of the words you read. Many of the strong words have lost their meaning. Love used to be a very potent word. People did not throw it about. But today we say: "I love God" or "I love my country" as non-chalantly as we say "I love pizza". Why? Because the word love has become so overused that it has lost its significance to selfishness and other human flaws.

Words are not uttered merely to exercise the mouth. The Bible states that death or life is in the power of your tongue. What you say is what you have. Yes, sometimes we may not see the results of our words immediately manifesting themselves in our lives but they will manifest eventually.

Many women who have recognized the potency of the their words early enough in life are now living a fulfilled life in God, enjoying their career, marriage and ministry, just by making positive confessions everyday of their lives.

Deciding to speak right words is crucial. It can make or break your life or the lives of people you speak to. So, what are the right things to say?

How do you make and keep the decision to say the right words?

First of all, you should not be guided by what you see or ear. Your eyes or ears are not the best advisors for your mouth. The right words may come out of your heart after being stimulated by your faith. After all the words of faith and love are the best. The world around us mostly offers negative information, which may prompt negative utterances. But the word of God and faith brings encouraging words to our lips.

Here is one of the golden rules to follow: the fewer, the better. You may not see many good things to say about something, but instead have plenty of bad ones. Make a decision to say few good words and stay away from saying the bad ones.

"Think twice before you speak, because your words and influence will plant the seed of either success or failure in the mind of another."

**Napoleon Hill**

"False words are not only evil in themselves, but they infect the soul with evil."

**Socrates**

# DECISION
# TO BE
# LOYAL

## 26. DECISION TO BE LOYAL

### "Through love and faithfulness sin is atoned for." - Proverbs 16:6

Loyalty is one great but rare quality nowadays. We live in a world of disposable things. This "disposable" mentality has shifted from things to people and relationships. We dispose of people at will when we do not need them anymore and loyalty has become a scarce commodity.

A couple who have lived together for forty years in marriage were once asked a question: "how did you manage to stay together so long?" You know what the answer was? They said: "in our time people used to fix things instead of throwing them away. So, making a decision to be loyal to someone, you find that perfect way to fix relationships or friendship instead of throwing them away."

If you get online and carry out a search on loyalty, you get such results as "how to build up your customer loyalty or brand loyalty". If you come across how to be a loyal person, it would most likely not be at the bottom of the search results. This is not a coincidence, it is an evidence of what the search engine's algorithm gets as most frequently search item on the subject. It shows that there are more people seeking loyalty form people than those who want to be loyal to people. It seems every one wants to have a loyal spouse, a loyal family, loyal friends, employees or customers. But how many people out there want to be loyal themselves?

Loyalty and love go hand in hand. Thus, a decision to be loyal is no fun. It takes guts to stay loyal to people in their times of trouble. So loyalty is best tested during tough times. It's easy to be loyal, when everything is alright. But what happens when things go sour? When the tree withers, the birds fly away to seek other places to build their nests.

The times of trouble are the best times to show loyalty to friends and family members. When we fail, we need love of others to cover up our sins and misfortunes and stand side by side with us to help make it through.

A decision to be loyal is rewarding. Once you stick through the storm with some people in your life, you become lifelong friends, because one loyal friend under the grey sky is worth more than a dozen who are around only when the weather is fair. Therefore, resolve to be a loyal friend, sister, daughter, niece, aunt, mother and wife. We value loyal people in our lives. We become willing to do much for them in the time of their need. So you see, loyalty pays back well. It is priceless indeed.

"Confidentiality is a virtue of the loyal, as loyalty is the virtue of faithfulness."

**Edwin Louis Cole**

"Loyalty and friendship, which is to me the same, created all the wealth that I've ever thought I'd have."

**Ernie Banks**

# DECISION
# TO BE
# DISCIPLINED

## 27. DECISION TO BE DISCIPLINED

**"Better a patient person than a warrior, one with self-control than one who takes a city." - Proverbs 16:32**

A decision to be disciplined is not an easy one, it takes a lot of hard work to attain. There is no way you can become disciplined unless you set your heart and mind on it and get to work. Discipline is about forming the right habits in your life. It's about becoming proactive and acting upon your decisions.

So, let's take a look at some practical tips that would help you to gain self-control and maintain your decision to be disciplined.

### STOP FIGHTING WITH YOUR OWN SELF

We all have inner struggles from time to time. But living in constant struggle is not healthy- especially with self. There is a part of you, which does not even want to hear of self-discipline. That part wants to stay lazy and do nothing to fix problems. You need to conquer yourself in that respect and not continue struggling. Your eyes will always tend to get drowsy, your back seeking a couch to lay on, your hands reaching for a cushion; even when duty beckons and stake are high. So, get up and take control of your body; tell it what to do, instead of indulging its excuse not to act.

### FIND STRONG MOTIVATION

Find something that would persuade the "lazy" part of you to move on and become disciplined. Do not leave that motivation to chances or to other people. Get yourself interested and excited about things you do and decisions you make. Yes, there are times when you need to press on no matter what. But there is no reason to turn your life into constant struggle.

Thin of the glorious results of high-flying women around, use it as a pointer to what you can achieve too and let that move you to action.

## REWARD YOURSELF

The Bible says that if we judged ourselves, there would be no need for others or for God to judge us. The same is true about rewarding or punishing ourselves. Set up pleasant rewards for carrying out your decision to be disciplined. And when you fail, you know you do not deserve the special treat.

## GUARD YOURSELF AGAINST DISTRACTIONS

Making a decision is not hard; sticking with it is the problem. It seems to be the way of life that when you make up your mind to do something, there comes many obstacles to derail you off track. Those are distractions. You have to stay fixed on your decision to keep them at bay.

## BECOME PROACTIVE

Once the decision is made, you need to begin being active. Do not sit and ponder your actions longer than you really need to. That is one of the key rules of self-discipline. Waiting won't get it done, acting will.

## GET RID OF FALSE IDEAS

Some people say: "being disciplined is not in my character". But as a woman , you are the primary caregiver of your home, and in effect the one who will account for the conduct of your children. If you do not inculcate discipline, how can you then pass it on? How would you break grounds and not be relegated in your career? Nobody is born self-disciplined or well organized. Discipline is a skill anyone can master; it's not hereditary. It is something you develop within the course of life. And when you do it successfully, it will reflect on everything that concerns you: your home will be a happy one, your career will record success, and your ministry will go from glory to glory.

Therefore, endeavour to adopt these guidelines to keep yourself on track in developing self-discipline, for by it, a great life will be yours for the taking.

"Work while you work, play while you play - this is a basic rule of repressive self-discipline."

**Theodor Adorno**

"With self-discipline most anything is possible."

**Theodore Roosevelt**

# DECISION TO ANTICIPATE

## 28. DECISION TO ANTICIPATE

**"Wait for the LORD, and he will avenge you." -
Proverbs 20:22**

Anticipation is a powerful tool for keeping yourself focused. Anticipation of good things will keep you watchful and take your eyes away from things you know will hinder you from getting it.

Anticipation is a neutral word. You may anticipate good things or bad things, the choice is yours. Anticipation is not just about the sensations you experience expecting things to happen. It has the power to stir your emotions, your thoughts and motivate you to certain words or actions.

You see, when you anticipate bad things, they tend to happen. It's not a coincidence. We say what we believe and we get what we say. By anticipating bad things, we talk of bad things and then act accordingly. We also become afraid. Fear either paralyzes us or makes us run. There are great chances you'd miss some opportunities in life, if you become guided by fear.

Thus, negative anticipation leads to negative reactions, triggering fear. On the contrary, positive anticipation keeps your spirits up. It's easy to stay happy, when you anticipate good things in life. Making a decision to anticipate good things, you change your attitude. You become more open to see chances that come your way in a positive light. Thus, you become strongly motivated to take those chances and use new opportunities in life to reach success.

Making a decision to anticipate good things you also start saying good things. Words have power. They determine the course of life. Plus, anticipating good things is a highly enjoyable experience. It is a good as getting the things themselves.

So, how do you go about the decision to anticipate good things? First of all, get control over what you hear or see. If you let too much negative information into your heart and mind, they form your anticipation. If you have trouble anticipating good things, think of good things, hear of good things, watch positive things, etc., and ponder on the negative.

Learn to boost up your anticipation of good things. This can be done through planning. Take tailored actions in preparations for it. If as a single woman, you are anticipating a great and blissful marriage, you position yourself for it. Knowing that you have a part to play, you read relevant books, cultivate godly and homely habits and work on your physical appearance among many other things. Why? Because you expect and have a full assurance that that will be your experience. Same goes for other endeavours in your life; if you truly anticipate them, you position yourself ahead, so that when they come your way, it does not get messed up in your hands. Remember how you used to anticipate holidays in your childhood? Try to refresh those feelings and learn how to stimulate them in practical ways.

> "Well," said Pooh, "what I like best," and then he had to stop and think. Because although eating honey was a very good thing to do, there was a moment just before you began to eat it which was better than when you were, but he didn't know what it was called."

> **A.A. Milne**

> "...anticipation of happiness can sometimes be as gratifying as its consummation."

> **Gaynor Arnold**

# DECISION TO TACKLE PROBLEMS

## 29. DECISION TO TACKLE PROBLEMS

**"Do not be wise in your own eyes; fear the LORD and shun evil." - Proverbs 3:7**

Have you ever had a small problem in your life, which has grown into a large problem just because you were slow to attend to it? Few problems come big into our lives. Most of them come small and then slowly grow, because we do not attend to them timely. We deny the reality of some, while we wallow in others. So, making a decision to promptly tackle problems is important.

Now, let's take a look at the things that hold us back from the timely tackling of problems.

### FEAR

Fear is a negative amplifier. It makes small things look big, especially if this fear has roots in your childhood. When a small problem comes into your life, and you become afraid of it, you give it a chance to grow further. Fear causes discomfort in your heart and mind, which results in you just closing your eyes towards the problem to avoid that discomfort. If the problem is small, it does disturb you for a while but it still lets you live comfortably on.

But once it matures with time, you suddenly open up your eyes to something even more disturbing and unpleasant. Now you have no way of shutting your eyes towards it. It suddenly dawns on you that you have to face it, but alas, it has grown tougher. Now it demands even more courage from you. Therefore, it's a good idea to develop a habit of dealing with small problems to prevent them from growing too big to handle.

## NEGLIGENCE

Some women just seem have a penchant for taking things lightly. You see your child developing strange habits like saying vulgar words, but say to yourself, 'he's just a child, he will grow up and learn'. But if you do not let him know that it's wrong, his peers will tell convince him that it's right; and in no time he will start carrying out the acts that those words are connected to. That is the possible result of negligence on a careless woman's part. If your work is taking a lot from form you such as your time, at th expense of your home, you should not be so negligent as to think it does not matter, everyone will be alright. Such attitude to problems may lead to catastrophic consequences. You know, if you deviate from your course just a little and keep going in this direction for a good while, you will never end up where you want to be.

## PROCRASTINATION

Postponing till tomorrow what you can do today is a total waste of time with dire consequences. You know you have a problem, but you think: I'll deal with it later. This later may never come; it may become harder or too late when you are finally ready. In fact, some people wait till the problem grows into monster, threatening their life, their home their health, before they attend to it with urgency. It becomes a case of emergency when it could have been avoided. When you postpone a addressing a problem for too long, it may become irreversible.

Now that you know the three top reasons problems escalate into disaster - fear, negligence and procrastination – you can make a firm decision to deal with them head-on and promptly.

"Intellectuals solve problems, geniuses prevent them."

**Albert Einstein**

"Within the covers of the Bible are the answers for all the problems men face."

**Ronald Reagan**

# DECISION TO OBEY

## 30. DECISION TO OBEY

**In all your ways submit to Him, and he will make your paths straight. - Proverbs 3:6**

Admittedly, the decision to obey is not the most popular one. Today we are all urged to be leaders, to take the initiative and to be active. Obedience sounds like a somewhat outdated word in the present world of Boss Proliferation. Pride has taken centre stage, pushing humility backstage. Still, obedience is the best choice in some situations. If you wish to know and take advantage of the blessings of obedience then read on.

The Bible tells us the obedience is the best sacrifice to God. That is what He loves the most in us. Why is that so? Well, just because obedience is the utmost form of trust and faith. You cannot willfully obey, if you do not trust the person in charge. While love is the root and lifeblood of faith, obedience is its ultimate evidence.

Sometimes the word "obedience" sounds almost equal to "abuse" in marriage. Women rebel against being obedient to their husbands. Why does this happen? Because the trust and love were broken in those marriages. At the root of disobedience as part of submission, is lack of faith (or trust, to be more appropriate). Few women would object submitting to husbands, who love them, as Christ loves the church. Few would disobey their husbands or be willing to die for them. Few women would be unhappy to submit to a wise and caring leadership of their men. If as a woman you find yourself in any of these situations- you do not feel loved enough, cared for- there are things you can do to bring yourself to obey.

First, check yourself. You see, it is easy to see the shortcomings of others while blind to our. But there is no smoke without fire, especially when your never used to be the way he is now. While doing the check, do so prayerfully. Ask God to reveal your faults to you and do that sincerely. You may be at fault in one way or the other, and you may not be. But whatever the case is, take the next step of having a sincere heart to heart conversation with your spouse. Approach this step prayerfully too. Remember that the effectual and fervent prayer of the righteous avails much. No sane husband who sees his wife's sincerity in making things work will not cooperate and try to turn a leaf to restore his relationship to normalcy.

Ultimately, having done your part, leave the process of restoration to God. However, you can only commit your ways to a God you obey. One truth about obedience is an evidence of a strained relationship. So, if you have hard time obeying God, this means your relationships with Him is not set right. Check your trust level. You are probably lacking in that area. You cannot truly say you obey God when you are disobedient to the people God has put in positions that you should obey and submit to. So, the whole issue of obedience vis-a-vis trust begins and ends with our relationship God. The same is true about other situations where obedience is called for.

You need to make a decision to obey your husband and your leaders, including spiritual leaders. If that decision is very hard for you to make, then you need to examine your heart and identify the root of your distrust. Sometimes, there are good reasons, maybe these people are unworthy of your trust. Regardless, God is always worthy of it. He will never fail you. He always has a plan to turn things around for you. So in any situation, making a decision to obey God is the best possible decision of all. When your obedience to Him is intact, He will walk you safely and successfully through your issue of obedience to other humans authorities.

"Obedience is the mother of success and is wedded to safety."

**Aeschylus**

"Obedience is an act of faith; disobedience is the result of unbelief."

**Edwin Louis Cole**

# DECISION
# TO BE
# YOU

## 31. DECISION TO BE YOU

**"Every word of God is flawless; he is a shield to those who take refuge in him." - Proverbs 30:5**

It's a decision each and every one of us has to make and keep every day of our life. Here is the truth you should ponder and learn: God has created you to be a unique person and He did not make a mistake in creating you. Growing up, we all experienced pressures as our society is fashion oriented and driven. People seem to esteem what is fashionable and some bits or parts of your personality may not fit into general definitions of what is ideal.

That is why lots of people out there dream of being someone else. They simply do not want to be themselves, not knowing that the more they try to be someone else, the more they lose the essence of who they are. They unconsciously deny their personalities, their bodies, their looks or their mind and their feelings. It's the reason we have so many idols in our days. Music idols, actors and actresses, politicians, etc. These idols are everywhere.

People become big fans of these idols, they worship them, they try to be like them, to look like them, to live like them. Women seem to be more guilty of this, since they have more flair for fashion. Now, if you worship the idols that your mind, your hands and your communities have made, you must know that both the idol and the one who worship them will abandon each other on that day of judgment (Isaiah 2:8 and 20).

Making a decision to be you is making a decision on who or what to worship. Now take a moment and think about who or what are your idols? Do you have any? They may be hard to recognize. But worshiping an idol always demands you to compromise part of your personality.

The world around us is always pressuring you to conform to another point of view. It wants you to meet its standards. There are so many women today who hate their bodies. They starve themselves almost to death just to meet someone else's standard of 'beauty'. But no matter how you look, or what you look like, if that is how God made you, then you are beautiful just the way you are.

If you dare to open up your eyes and see things for what they are, you begin to see the madness of those worldly idols. They always want you to be someone else and make you buy things or pay for things you have no use for. But God is not like that. He hates sin, but loves people and He has created you to be a unique person with your unique God given personality. He never intends for you to change that. He loves you the way you are. And He made you that way, He intends it as the best way to ensure you bring out the best in you to His glory. He intends for you to shine in your spot, not under another person's light.

If you embrace you the way you are today, you will notice a change in your confidence level. You have begin to worry less because you are no longer bothered about impressing people. You will get so busy bringing out the best of you and in you, manifesting God's glory.

"Be yourself, let you come through."

**Jonathan Davis**

"If you can just be yourself, then you have to be original because there's no one like you."

**Marc Newson**

365 Brilliant English Words

# OTHER BOOKS BY
# ABRAHAM GREAT

∎

## 31 Decisions that make a man of value

## 31 Decisions that make a Woman of Value

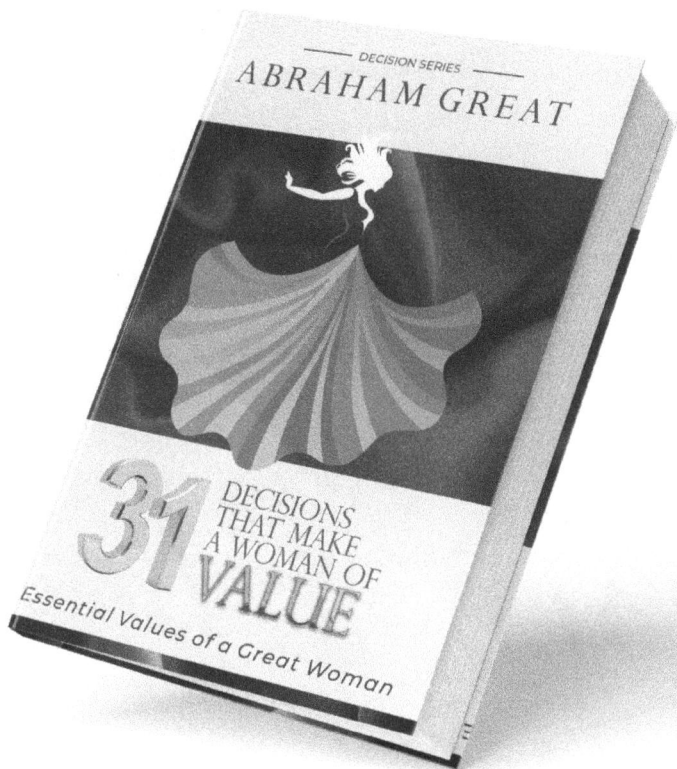

**OTHER BOOKS BY**
# ABRAHAM GREAT

## Understanding Values

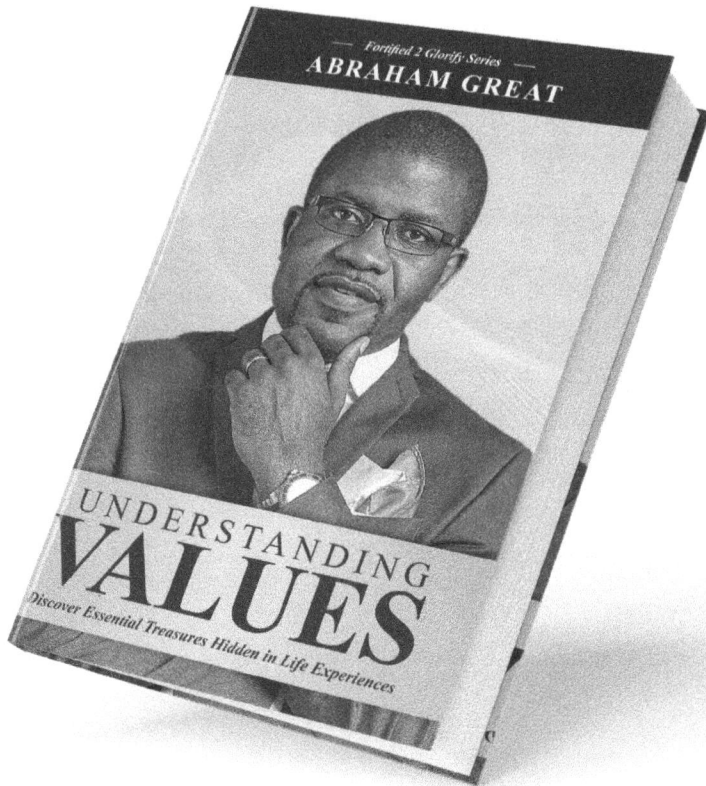

Fortified 2 Glorify Series
ABRAHAM GREAT

UNDERSTANDING
VALUES
Discover Essential Treasures Hidden in Life Experiences

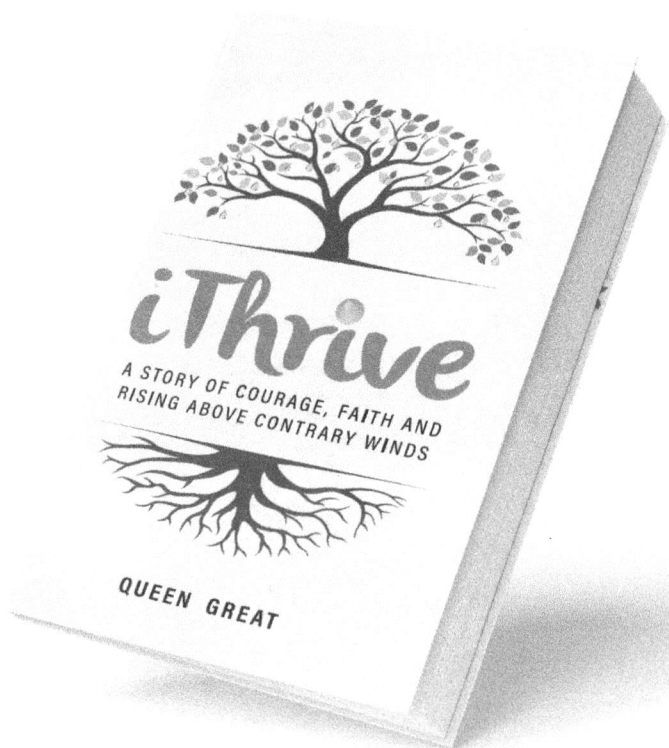

www.ingramcontent.com/pod-product-compliance
Lightning Source LLC
Chambersburg PA
CBHW030311100426
42812CB00002B/656